Praise for *Ants on the Melon*
by Virginia Hamilton Adair

"Virginia Adair speaks directly and unaffectedly, in an accent stripped of mannerism and allusion. *Ants on the Melon* exhibits enough formal variety, freshness and intelligence to confirm, at one stroke, that Ms. Adair is a poet of accomplishment and originality."

—BRAD LEITHAUSER, *The New York Times Book Review*

"Extraordinarily moving. Her voice is clear, assured, varied, and utterly her own."

—A. ALVAREZ, *The New York Review of Books*

"The rhyme is ingenious, the humor saucy and unsparing, and the author clearly takes a delight in perversity, in an inversion of the expected."

—ALICE QUINN, *The New Yorker*

"The poems in *Ants on the Melon* are beautifully organized to show the translucent layers of meaning and ways of seeing that were added to the steadfast, dead-on voice of Adair's poetry with each new life experience, each move and each new place."

—*Los Angeles Times*

"The distinctive voice of a woman who has seen most of the century and who gives powerful testimony to its global and intimate details—from meditations on nuclear war to those on widowhood—is a gift. The publication of her book is a literary event."

—THOMAS LYNCH (National Book Award nominee), *The Detroit Free Press*

"Virginia Adair is indeed a major discovery."

—*St. Louis Post-Dispatch*

"How bright and unmuddled and unaffected and unswerving these poems are. There's such aplomb, no faking, such a hard true edge. They never miss."

—ALICE MUNRO

"Adair writes with a thinking heart's and a feeling mind's unusual clarity. Here is a sensual, wise, precise, amazing voice."

—SHARON OLDS

"Tart, knowledgeable poems by a woman who has lived long and felt deeply. They surprise and delight us with their passion."

—MAXINE KUMIN

"She is very, very, very good, the fine, agile turn like an arabesque on ice that blasts, lightning-like, into a ghastly abyss."

—E. ANNIE PROULX

"Virginia Adair's poems are startling, funny, erotic, tragic, wise, sometimes all these at once. With what wit and intelligence she awakens the ordinary world. She has arrived in our world like a comet."

—GALWAY KINNELL

ANTS ON THE MELON

ALSO BY VIRGINIA HAMILTON ADAIR

Beliefs and Blasphemies

ANTS ON THE MELON

A Collection of Poems

VIRGINIA HAMILTON ADAIR

THE MODERN LIBRARY

NEW YORK

1999 Modern Library Paperback Edition

Copyright © 1996 by Virginia Hamilton Adair

All rights reserved under International and
Pan-American Copyright Conventions. Published in
the United States by Random House, Inc., New York,
and simultaneously in Canada by Random House
of Canada Limited, Toronto.

Modern Library and colophon are registered trademarks of Random House, Inc.

This work was published in hardcover by Random House, Inc. in 1996.

Some of the poems that appear in this work were originally published in the following:
*Atlantic Monthly, Best Poems (Borestone), Beyond Baroque, Claremont Quarterly, College
English, A Garland for John Berryman, Michigan Quarterly, Mount Holyoke Quarterly, The
New Republic, The New Yorker, New York Quarterly, Poet Lore, Road Apple, Southern
Humanities Review, Stonecloud, Western Humanities Review, Western Review,* and *Wormwood.*

Library of Congress Cataloging-in-Publication Data
Adair, Virginia, 1913–
Ants on the melon : a collection of poems / Virginia Hamilton
Adair. — Modern Library ed.
p.   cm.
ISBN 0-375-75229-3 (acid-free paper)
1. Title.
PS3551.D244A82   1999
811'.54—dc21   98-52069

Modern Library web site address: www.modernlibrary.com

Printed in the United States of America

BVG 001

To Robert Browning Hamilton (1880–1974)
and to Robert Mezey

in gratitude

Contents

ANTS ON THE MELON

Key Ring / 3
Summary by the Pawns / 4
Asbury Park, 1915 / 5
Fordham Road, 1917 / 7
The Grandmothers / 8
Early Walk / 10
The Shell / 11
The April Lovers / 12
Railway Tempo / 13
Musical Moment / 14
An Hour to Dance / 15
Drowned Girl / 16
Cor Urbis / 18
The Dark Hole / 20
The Survivors / 22
Ants on the Melon / 25

BY OLD MAPS

Yorktown Ferry / 29
Buckroe, After the Season, 1942 / 30

By Old Maps / 32

Narrow Gauge / 34

LAX–Gatwick / 35

Return / 37

Grasmere Journal / 38

Americans in Bloomsbury / 40

English Visit / 42

Nocturne / 44

Windmill Time / 45

In Dublin's Fair City, 1963 / 46

Reunion Between Planes / 48

Now You Need Me / 49

Blackened Rings / 50

DRIVING WESTWARD

The Trek / 55

Laguna in September / 56

Surfers / 58

Winter Zendo / 60

Riding a Koan / 62

Light in Wrightwood / 64

Driving Westward / 66

Godstone / 68

Mojave Evening / 70

Abandoned Anthill / 71

Two of Us / 72

Yea, Though I Walk / 73

Second Coming / 75

Sonoran Cattle / 76

Withdrawal / 78

THE GENESIS STRAIN

The Genesis Strain / 81
God to the Serpent / 84
TV Brideshead Revisited / 85
Cutting the Cake / 87
Child as Deity / 88
The Wedding Frame / 89
Home Notes / 91
Pity Ulysses / 93
Too Small for Words / 94
In Nomine / 96
Corona Fidei / 98
Now We Lay Us / 100
Strange Frequency / 101

EXIT AMOR

Where Did I Leave Off? / 105
Peeling an Orange / 107
Blueberry City / 108
By the Waters / 110
Firewind / 112
One Ordinary Evening / 113
Dark Lines / 115
The Ruin / 116
Exit Amor / 117
The Year After / 118
Coronach / 119
A Last Marriage / 120
Two Sides of the Coin / 122
Fair Warning / 125
Midstairs / 127

Return to Madison / 131
Red Camellias / 133
For Scholar-Poets R.M. and R.G.B. / 135
John Berryman's Winter Landscape / 136
Shirley / 137
Lorna / 139
Pilot / 141
Dover / 143
Slow Scythe / 145
Strings / 146
Break In / 148
White Darkness / 149
Take My Hand, Anna K. / 150

AFTERWORD / 151

ANTS ON THE
MELON

Key Ring

When my grandfather was very old
to one small room confined
he gave me his big bunch of keys to hold.

I asked, "Do they unlock every door there is?
And what would I find inside?"

He answered, "Mysteries and more mysteries.
You can't tell till you've tried."

Then as I swung the heavy ring around
the keys made a chuckling sound.

Summary by the Pawns

First the black square, then a white,
Moved by something out of sight,

We are started with a bound,
Knights and castles all around,
Kings and queens and bishops holy!

After that we go more slowly,
While around us with free gaits
Move the taller potentates.

Still we pawns look straight ahead.

To encourage us it's said
That pawns who reach the utmost square
Are as good as monarchs there.

Meanwhile pawns, if need be, can
By slanted ways remove a man;

But frequently, before we know
What has got us, off we go!

Asbury Park, 1915

I
I am two-and-a-half-years-old,
hand in hand between my parents.
"What is that big thing?"
"A cannon?" says my father.
The cannon sits on its two wheels and tail
in a sea of red flowers.
"Roses," I say.
"No," says my mother, "those are cannas."
In a burst of delight I chant,
        "She looked at the canna
        and jim-jamma-jane."
It is my first poem.
My mother wants to know,
"Do you mean 'cannon' or 'canna'?"
But on the picture-postcard of my mind,
cannons and red flowers
are forever one.

II

In a white muslin dress and piqué hat
barefoot on the sea's edge,
I dismiss parental warnings.
"The Atlantic Ocean can't drown ME!"
Heading for the horizon
I walk into the shallow foam.
Mother in a long linen skirt
and red shoes with French heels,
splashes into the surf and yanks me shoreward.
We emerge wet and indignant.
My father with his accordion-pleated Kodak
preserves the scene on sepia film.

For almost eighty years
we have stood there on the sand,
safe from the sea, in a black album.

Fordham Road, 1917

small watchman
from a Bronx window
I marveled at beards and kerchiefs
alien voices and gestures
flooding my birth-city

They put down their bundles
they peel the first banana

I call back across wars and seven decades
dear strangers, forgive me now
that I did not hug your knees
signifying gratitude
that out of all the world you chose
our coast for your landing

Has it been a good move?
You would not go back?

The Grandmothers

As widows in their fifties
they donned black, my grandmothers:
high-necked, tight-waisted, corseted,
silk for Sundays, crepe for afternoons,
checkerboard black and white
for morning duties; ebony cross
with pearls, a gold watch pinned
on the chest, a birthstone brooch,
black shoes, black hose, black veils,
black god-knows-what-else never seen.
Oh, there might be a silver fox
with black, black eyes and nose
over the shoulders, and in puffs and coils
of silver hair, thick combs of tortoiseshell
not quite so black, but dark.

Black was the ribbon on the wreath
that hung on the door for the husband
newly dead. Handkerchiefs were edged
in black, notepaper had a border
of black to signal widowhood.

But they were merry, my grandmothers.
Their mirth flowed over at a jest,
a child's naiveté, the ways
of the sultanic black cat, Blackamoor.
I see one at the piano: "Liebestod"
romps into "Maple Leaf Rag,"
her black toe tapping.
I see the other at the backyard pump
with a bowl of surplus pancakes
for the birds: orioles, tanagers,
jays and cardinals, wild with color
and competition. I hear her cries
of laughter as her blacksleeved arms
hold the hotcakes aloft
among the dip and swirl of brilliant wings.

Early Walk

On my early walk
I passed the Frog Prince
dead in a rut of the road

his lordly legs spread out
for a royal leap
plump thighs
a fan of tapering toes

his shapely body
flattened
by a passing wheel

and, in a long and purple flume,
like a worm in the wet sand
his gut forlorn.

The Shell

On the desolate border between the living land
And land lying entombed under the sea,
The littered and soaking sand
Strewn with wrecked wood and clotted moss

Which the waves continually toss,
Toss, and then regather into the foam and swell,
I saw, shapely and thin, with delicate gloss
And strangely spiraled, a wan shell.

A shell delicate and turned without fault,
Pale, icy, thin as despair,
Washed in the dead bitterness of salt
It was born in the sea,

Torn from the sea into the air.
Some other may lift it from the sand;
I do not dare. Never has my hot hand
Held any substance so desolate and so rare.

The April Lovers

Green is happening.
Through the sweet expectant chill
Of a northern spring
We have gone without will,

Without fear, without reason,
Trusting to the power
Of a fickle season,
Of a passionate hour,

To mature, to sustain
Till the plan uncovers
In the sun and rain.
Early lovers

Never question much
What is quietly beating
Through the music and the touch
And the mouths meeting.

Railway Tempo

Now vanish, nameless village, tossed
Into the oblivion of our wake.

Swiftly, the high road that we crossed
And blotted out, the lake, the thickets,
And the wide meadow, for our sake
—We being arbiters of time
Whose end is punched on one-way tickets—
These idle images must recede
Beyond our sphere of plush and grime.

For we, the here and now, command
Collapse to follow our fierce speed,
And only the final town to stand.

Musical Moment

Always the caravan of sound made us halt
to admire the swinging and the swift go-by
of beasts with enormous hooves and heads
beating the earth or reared against the sky.

Do not reread, I mean glance ahead to see
what has become of the colossal forms:
everything happened at the instant of passing:
the hoof-beat, the whinny, the bells on the harness,
the creak of the wheels, the monkey's fandango
in double time over the elephant's back.

When the marching was over and we were free to go on
there was never before us a dungfall or a track
on the road-sands of any kind:
only the motion of footprints being made
crossing and recrossing in the trampled mind.

An Hour to Dance

For a while we whirled
over the meadows of music
our sadness put away in purses
stuffed into old shoes or shawls

the children we never were
from cellars and closets
attics and faded snapshots
came out to leap for love
on the edge of an ocean of tears

like a royal flotilla
Alice's menagerie swam by
no tale is endless
the rabbit opened his watch
muttering late, late
time to grow
old

Drowned Girl

Face the drowned girl, whose fighting limbs and breath
the profound wave silenced with cool images:

Look, here's the first round world, equipped with warmth
and a wise nipple knowing your needs. See next
a million children hard at play; your feet
the fastest, your fist triumphant, your fingers thieving
bright apples from their counterpoint of leaves.

"See here," said the wave, and urged her dreaming body
down surging stairs of gloom deepward; "I divulge
the bee-stretched flower, the honey winging home,
a singing dot in the pure silences."

And so, corrupted by the dear story, her heart
gave over its rhythm to the sea's monody. She gave
her white body for a chord in the dirge of herself
and twice reclimbed the cloudy stair for ecstasy
of slow descent through failures and desires.

No push of pulse, no battle in the blood
finally disturbed the saline melody
when last the swell through dissonance of surf
bore her, loose-fingered and with heavy hair,
to resolution on the empty shore.

O listen for the notes, the last white chord
struck trailing on the sand, before it brings
the curious and the screams; face the drowned girl
before the blanket comes, and the grave men.

Cor Urbis

Over the suicidal approaches
Where guns have human eyes
And even the ozone stoops to murder
   I will speed you to the heart
   the heart of the great city.

Along the varicose thoroughfares
Paved with the worst intentions
Where *stop* and *go* are poverty and power
   I will lead you to the heart
   the heart of the great city.

Among foul nets of streets straining
To contain defilement and despair
Where the facades ooze and peel like scabs
   I will pull you to the heart
   the heart of the great city.

Into a black hall where couples
Copulate against the wall
Up stairways puked and pissed upon
   I will show you the full heart
   the heart of the great city.

And so to the cubicle of stench
Past rats running for offices
Roaches and flies feeding like bankers
   We come fast to the heart
   the heart of the great city.

Down in the lidless ring of the bowl
Behold a dead blue face
Fetus enthroned in rust and blood
   Here at last is the heart
   the heart of the great city.

The Dark Hole

Douglass the third is three.
He is digging a hole in the sand on the beach at Nags Head.
Nearby is Kitty Hawk, where our first plane
flew for a few hundred yards.
Another name is in the air: Hiroshima,
a bomb dropping. It sounds like the ocean wind;
but the voices are strange, triumphant and horrified.
He has no words yet for this mixture of tones.
"Does this mean the war has ended?" he asks.
"Yes." "Who won?"
"We did," his mother tells him. "We have the bomb."

Days later his mother is ironing.
She asks him, "Will you go up to the dark hole
and bring me three coat hangers?
They're in a box at the door."
The dark hole is their name for the windowless attic.
Douglass asks, "Do I have to go?"
"No, but you always like to be helpful."
"I'll go," he says.

Twenty years later they both recall the incident.
"When you said we had the atomic bomb," he tells her,
"I thought you meant our family did.
I thought it must be in the dark hole."
He had thought at first it must all be an accident,
like when you dropped something you didn't mean to:
you were ashamed, and sometimes punished.
Fifty years later we still have no words
for the confusion of jubilation and horror,
for the agony of bodies with flesh hanging in tatters
from their shoulder bones;
triumphant, the secret fruit of Oak Ridge
had ripened, falling from a single plane
on an unsuspecting town.
Pity for the three-year-old climbing the stairs
with silent courage
into the terror of catastrophe,
into the dark hole where, yes,
our entire nation owned and kept the fire-wind
of Hiroshima, Nagasaki, the atolls and islands,
the pasturelands of Utah, other remote and quiet
playing fields of a nonexistent war.

The Survivors

All of earth's men are on the march somewhere.
Out of two stolen continents depart
The sons of heaven and the supermen;
Mirages take the maps; none can refind
The way he came; the herded slave, once more
A man, repeats the names of vanished towns;
The bearded skeleton sees an unknown world
Beyond the wire, through layers of vertigo,
Where roofless women push their carts and children
To the last ditch beyond the famished farm;
Exiles still seek, through the indifferent nations,
A halt, a habitation, and a smile.

Blessed citizen of a country still uncharred,
Our cast-off worker reconverts to hunger;
Hunts through the critical cities for a sign.
Even our soldier, banished in such glory
To set the world to rights, looks in a daze
Down to the dock and the returning transport;
Relaxes his hazy purpose and his fear:
Tries to remember, was home there, or here.

War's hated and intense environment
Shared by unshaven misery through shock
And deprivation and profane endurance
Now as he leaves it no less hated still
Reclaims him darkly; clamors in his head:

This despised earth received his excrement,
Yielded him brackish water for his throat
And burning body; took his exact weight
In fever and in sleep and while he fed;
Buried his fear for him in sodden holes
Beneath the iron singing and fall of shells.
Here too his brothers lie, rebuild the soil;
And but for some ballistic error, here lies he.

The soldier asks, "This transport take me back?
Back where? What map can show the point
To which I can return and call my home?"

Arrived, he shuts the door, with a half-smile
Faces the room of past, well-dusted peace.
Doubt waits at doors, hums at the windy eaves,
Hides sleepless in the dry leaves, slyly enters
The echoes and the silence of his bed,
Hinting, this is not home. Departure, not return,
His lot forever now if he would find
Where the center has shifted to. For some will search
And some will shut the door and marry doubt.

All men are now survivors of one hour
When by their knowledge and their desperate need
They split the unseen, indivisible core
Of God and matter, scattering their last belief.
Scientist, soldier, worker, preacher, planner
Fall in with all men henceforth on the march
Within themselves, imploring passage home.

1945

Ants on the Melon

Once when our blacktop city
was still a topsoil town
we carried to Formicopolis
a cantaloupe rind to share
and stooped to plop it down
in their populous Times Square
at the subway of the ants

and saw that hemisphere
blacken and rise and dance
with antmen out of hand
wild for their melon toddies
just like our world next year
no place to step or stand
except on bodies.

BY
OLD
MAPS

Yorktown Ferry

Again the carload of children
the sharp landing bell and the foam
between us and the low shore.
Our breath was taken by the wind's fanfare,
performing clouds, great ferries
and small craft greeting on the watery
midway, bright things flapping
gulls like calliopes and the sun
breaking up in laughter
over the clowning waves

And coming home, the children
singing or sleeping, the mystery
of moongold and boatlights flaring
on the black mirror of the York
the wait at the landing the bump
the rumbling off-and-aboard of cars
and then departure into that
ancient tide long since spanned
with steel: no feeling now the soft
swell, the profound river sigh.

Buckroe, After the Season, 1942

Past the fourth cloverleaf, by dwindling roads
At last we came into the unleashed wind;
The Chesapeake rose to meet us at a dead end
Beyond the carnival wheels and gingerbread.

Forsaken by summer, the wharf. The oil-green waves
Flung yellow foam and sucked at disheveled sand.
Small fish stank in the sun, and nervous droves
Of cloud hastened their shadows over bay and land.

Beyond the NO DUMPING sign in its surf of cans
And the rotting boat with nettles to the rails,
The horse dung garlanded with jeweling flies
And papers blown like a fleet of shipless sails,

We pushed into an overworld of wind and light
Where sky unfettered ran wild from earth to noon,
And the tethered heart broke loose and rose like a kite
From sands that borrowed diamonds from the sun.

We were empty and pure as shells that air-drenched hour,
Heedless as waves that swell at the shore and fall,
Pliant as sea-grass, the rapt inheritors
Of a land without memory, where tide erases all.

By Old Maps

The winter of our long search
for Rosewell, we followed ghosts
of buried roads through cornfields,
perplexed in a panorama
of unpeopled fields and copses.

Time and again we halted
in the place where it had to be:
the great house, the legend. Saw
only the crows, ploughed areas,
a few vine-hung islands of trees.

Went by water, walked inland
to the same clearing, staring
while the wind said "No, it is not
a mirage." Vast creepers cumbered
the towering walls. A tarnkappe*
of leaves hid windows, stairwells.
Forest trees embraced in the hall.

*The "hat of darkness" given to Siegfried
in the *Nibelungenlied*. It renders its wearer
invisible.

As we moved into this tangle
of time, daffodils frolicked
at our feet in surges of light
from what long-sleeping beauty's
touch, on the lawns once emerald?

Narrow Gauge

Tony, remember our ride,
Richmond to Lynchburg, Virginia,
on the small woodburning train?
Four cars ran on the narrow rails
through sunset fields
dotted white with dogwood.

The dining car? Our conductor
smiled. "If you hungry, we wire
ahead to a widow lady, fixes
a fine box supper for you-all."

At one stop we lost a coach,
at one we ran forward, climbed
to the woodsmoke cab of the kingly
engineer, waved on by childhood.
At dusk two boxes came aboard:
fried chicken, cupcakes, strawberries.

How long since that folktale ride
across five counties? Descending
in the night, we found that ours
was the final and the only car.

LAX–Gatwick

I
Flying alone between a hot oasis
and a cool island, nine hours, six miles high,
over sierras, tundra, seas of sky,
my mind staggers: I know not what this place is—
no map, no mirror to tell me what my face is—
anonymous as a myth, I fly and fly.
And who can say on landing, who *am* I,
emerging dazed from this tumultuous stasis?

Yes, I will gather from the evidence
my baggage offers, and my teeming purse,
a date and place of birth, a name, a nation,
my sex, my current worth (in pounds and pence),
passport identity. For better or worse,
none checks the soul, nor asks its destination.

II
Speeding into the dark, Las Vegas gone,
the grandest canyon filled with shifting cloud,
into my ears piped music rushes loud,
drowning the jets that hurl me into dawn.
Small ancient men crouched in an earlier dawn
and watched the smoke rise in an arcane cloud,
then stamping, chanting, heads thrown back or bowed,
beheld hot metal tears drawn from the stone.

The Age of Bronze yields to a rage of wings.
I, ignorant of the early miners' lore,
climb effortless undreamed-of steeps of air.
Metal I cannot name ascends and sings,
while in its intricate womb I crouch and soar
beyond my power to know what brought me there.

Return

After a few centuries
we prodigals came home in August.

London lowered her skies.
The fatted calf withdrew
into sullen pasties.
People in pubs backed off.
We had lived among swine.

Only the small country churches
opened their dim doors to us
like ancient aunts.
Half blind, they mistook us
for their lost congregations.

Grasmere Journal*

(May 14–June 7, 1800)

He has taken my speechless kiss and gone
To his Mary now in the middle of May.
I sate a long time upon a stone
He will bring her back as a bride some day.

I capture the wind and the small rain,
The rhythms of work, the evening quiet.
I shall give William pleasure by it
When he comes home again.

I plant and hoe for the distant yield
But without his warmth the day is raw.
I turned aside at my favourite field,
My heart dissolved in what I saw.

Weather and sky and all I feel,
The love, the loneliness, the lake
With spear-shaped streaks of polished steel
Are an offering for William's sake.

*Lines and phrases in italics are direct quotations
from Dorothy Wordsworth's *Journal.*

On his return will he confess
That our haven here from the world's din
Calls home the heart to quietness?
I could not keep the tears within.

The skobby sate quietly in its nest.
But I labor long and listen late
Till my heart leaps up and the hour is blest
With William's hand on the trembling gate.

He's home. The Grasmere fills the sky
And my brimming love can ask no more
Than this *dance of spirits* bounded by
Its small circumference of shore.

Americans in Bloomsbury

One empty Sunday
on all fours
in the soot
of Bedford Street
we were rubbing
coal-hole covers
with cobblers' wax
and shelf paper

when this black preacher
halted over us
crying Praise God
our young folks
down on their knees!
The Lord given you
eyes to see!
He was from Tampa.

Two Londoners
with a woolen child
appalled
and fearing converse
crossed
to the other side
with small glances
like pigeon droppings.

English Visit

When we came to the country place of Jack Morpurgo
it had a moat, by God, a dry moat.
Jack hosted us in through a massive portal, groaning
on black hinges big as battleships.
Our breath was white ice in the rugless hall:
stones scooped and softened by centuries of shoes—
boot, buskin, slipper, sandal, patten, clog.
"In here," said Jack, opening a paneled door
on relative warmth where a fire cavorted over
the torso of a forest giant. Who hauled it in?
Not the white hands of bookish Jack Morpurgo
or his wife, the actress Kay, who knelt on the hearth
to stir a hissing jug with a hot poker.

I crooked my neck at the ceiling in disbelief;
hundreds of carven squares and each unique.
Awestruck I lay on my back, the better to look.
"Others have done the same before," said Jack.
"This was a king's hunting lodge; fourteen-
something, we think. Some bloody Henry or other."
Firelight flattered the ancient patterning
As I stared at the unsigned masterwork above,
Kay set a steaming mug beside my hand;
But what was this chill as if from underground?—
a royal spectre passed in vair and velvet
and kicked me lightly, taking me for his hound.

Nocturne

Draw the hour
dark as a bruise

where neon shopfronts
jerk and implore

on-off, arrow-arrow
enter me, like any whore.

On streets of soot and stain
the first brushes of rain

daub jewels and holocausts
through violet exhausts

and the wet deepens like a dream
while souls in stereo

ferry the black and fiery stream.

Windmill Time

Along the Norfolk Broads
the windmills are dying,
their monkish caps blown away,
their crossed arms broken.

In the churches, too, with beams
eaten by worm and beetle
the cross is only a curiosity.
The arms of Christ are broken.

Wind bending the reeds apart,
sails travel the old route
to the sea. Thistledown crosses
the wide water. Inland, lorries

wrapped in their own fumes
rumble down roads to no place.
Across the sky soft clouds
of England erase time,

time as we still name it
Anno Domini. Passing we stare
at churches where no one kneels
and windmills lost to the wind.

In Dublin's Fair City, 1963

City of hunger and sorrow
the contempt of your conquerors
colors the streets grey.
Your wars are never won.
A grimy rain prevails
like tears of the defeated
or the famous indignation of Swift
dampening forever the Dublin stones.

In his library near the cathedral
the collection is the same
as when Swift climbed the stairs
to those austere ranges
leather and gold bindings closed
on his scurrilous marginalia.
A frozen scholar or two crouches
in the coffin smell of wood.
The librarian like Keats's hare
limps trembling.

Only in the shabby pubs
or on desperate trolley-cars
the crazy Irish mirth crackles into words.
We should get off here, I say
this is our stop.
No, not yet, says my husband.
There, there, cry the crones in chorus
the man is always right, dearie.
Even God won't let us get off
till he pulls the bell.

Dublin, city of sighing rain
Joyce did well to map and mock you
from a blind distance.
Even the prism of Yeats's dream
fails to alleviate the grey, the grime.

Reunion Between Planes

I'm the old schoolfriend
swooping out of the sky
like a Halloween witch
in my Hollywood shades
and my stretchable wig
and a girdle of groans.
Since we shrieked our goodbyes
in a shower of rice
my babies have grown beards
been jailed and divorced.
My husband the broker
embezzled, absconded,
is living abroad with
a kennel of bitches.
I remember your dad
who fondled our bottoms
your mom with her bottle
she hid in the sofa.
My god, they were younger
by decades than we are
crossing into the dusk
of this terminal bar.

Now You Need Me

When the rains come
you remember
our old closeness
humping along
in the wet.
You grope the dark
where I hang
morosely
by my crooked neck.
You pull off my cover
shake me till my
ribs jiggle
and a moth flies out.
Your hand reaches under
my black skirt
and up one leg
thin as a cane
until I open wide
with a rusty squawk
hovering above you
like a dark and loving
raven, said the old
umbrella, her night
full of holes.

Blackened Rings

Once, to come so far
up tilted prairies to the mile-high
beginning of the barrier peaks
was to cry farewell until death do us join
to all the faces
the little fences of the East.

Between the tears on the homespun blanket
and the deafening silence of the stars
the alder-smoke marked time westward:
each blackened ring spelled sleep.

And the day started with a puff of frost
the sigh and sign of waking.
I came, I saw,
but the conquering took a long time.

Out of the bones of young men
the lodgepole pine;
out of the girl who groaned
entering her final stillness
the alder yielded its bark to the winter deer
branches for lonely fires
and a slight song of leaves.

Now to return is not impossible
the slow wheels having grown wings;
but my blood tells me that the trail ends here
at the vast waters of the sleeping sun.

How should I turn again past death
past life, go down the grainlands
to that narrower sea?
finding the dreams have faces
and the places fences
and myself a mere hovering
spun of some traveler's frosty breath
he pausing
high on the crest
of one of the great passes
looking for the last time
both east and west.

DRIVING
WESTWARD

The Trek

We are all leaders
whom nobody follows

only the selves inside
the shadowy marchers

crossing the dead trails
surprising a pair of eyes

stopping by cold fires
or calling across the canyon

hello   echo   hello

I have brought my company
to this edge, this falling off

hello   hello

Laguna in September

Slow surf traces
with luminous chalk
the seal-brown ledges.

From your fingers
waves of clear music.

Under a heaving surface
the bronze reefs.

What is the color of a name?

Bougainvillea pours vivid
over pale cliffs
the sun bursts like a balloon.

From the stone-blue horizon
of this sea I turn

I strain to see you
prince of your trees and lawns
of eastern green.

High over tidepool rocks
wings splinter the sky
and veer descending;

I hear the faraway cry
of your winter axe.

Surfers

Four half-grown figures start
down the precipitous headland
hung with crimson ice plant.
Ceremonial as a crucifer,
each with his surfboard raptly faces
the blue-mauve insomnia of the sea.

They place their boards like prayer rugs
kneeling with reverent grace
to the messianic wave
forever watched for
forever coming.

With tireless love
they offer their frailty
to that hypnotic vastness,
oaring with their arms
toward the horizon whence comes their hope.

Around their heads
the sun makes halos of gold and ivory;

angels of water and air
bless them, test them
with blows, perils, and at last,
after a few passionate seasons
wooing the god,
will crucify their youth
on the bright headland where new converts
pass them without pity
watching for the wave.

Winter Zendo

Upward in silence through fresh snow
under the night sky we moved
and the conifer branches moved,
shifted snow a little, and the stars
moved shifting light, and ahead
the leader's lantern moved.

So we came to the dark zendo
and discarded heavy boots and shoes.
Now barefoot on bare boards
we paced into that icy hall
to sit, legs folded, on the long shelf,
our hands a basket tilting outward.

Then self from the tilted basket spilled
like bodiless sand and dropless water
into the nothingness of the night.
Our elbows pressed against our sides
created warmth, while each breath
mingled with the sweet breath of incense.

I can sit in a summer room alone,
narrow my eyes and in an instant
feel the snow underfoot, the stir
of stars and branches; I abandon
the heavy footgear, heavy thoughts,
to enter again that silence and strange joy.

The wooden clappers startle; the bell
widens its circles till the tone passes
beyond the body's power to hear,
beyond the illusory pulse of time,
while the mind moves outward on these expanding
invisible and soundless rings.

At last the drum leads our chanting
in a lost tongue the impossible vows:
above all to save all sentient creatures
from suffering. No throne of judgment;
only compassion for all, from all;
for all are one, one in the mind of God.

SHU JO MU HEN SEI GAN DO*

*"However innumerable beings are, I vow to save them."

Riding a Koan

My koan waits
unsaddled, unbridled
tied to nothing.

I mount and ride
out of the map
into a tangle of stars.

Currents of grass
move through me,
and the scented rain.

I peer through snow
dust, fire, tornadoes,
into the vulture's eye.

Suns stampede
cantering through me
in my thicket of bones.

My koan whisks away
flies and words
finally, itself.

The earth opens
like a beak
through which I sing.

Alone on the prairie now
sod to cut
a well to dig.

Light in Wrightwood

Light on silicon dust
needles of Jeffrey pine
ripe cherries, foil
to keep off crested jays
(they find this hilarious)
light on high bare slopes
where the snows slip down
into desert summer

Light on the threshold
of this old cabin, survivor
of earthquakes, mudslides,
ten-foot snows, where I stand
survivor of seventy summers,
winters, avarice done with
and so much still to love

Light on the thinning hair
of my grown children
faces of their growing children
light on the hands of friends
waving hello, goodbye
car bumping down the canyon road

Light resting on treetops
in this upland valley
a wind that comes with darkness
high branches waving
goodbye, farewell, good night

O, ritual smell of woodsmoke
deadwood giving its last light

Driving Westward

Age, grief, perversities
of lovers and investments
vanish in the exhalation
of our speed or, hydrocarbon
ghosts, hover beyond tinted glass.

Points of departure and destination
are folded away in paper maps
when we enter the 4-lane fairyland
swinging like bells
for some nameless jubilee.

Who has not known as driver
before the bright controls
this hubris of the freeway
this rapture of the horizontal
plunge into receding sanity?

Here at our slightest touch
musicians hanging in the wind
spend, spend their sweetness
into our cells of chrome and foam
our lives their opera.

The slow God shepherding
his clouds across blue pastures
dissolves before our eyes
the land unrolls like doomsday
and all our coffins fly into the sun.

Godstone

This handsize rock inhabits
the outline of itself
on the sand. Its weight
is itself, not pressing
or lifting. It possesses
only a long lineage
of mountain, lava, planet,
showers of space
and a selfbombing star.
It looks neither ahead
nor pastward. It is mooncold,
noonhot, windburnished,
its underside melon dusk
of a wintersunset.
Sands settle around it
and colonies of seeds
waiting for the rare rain.
The lizard uses it as a plaza.
Ants cross it carrying
their dead and perhaps mine.
The sun plays shadowgames
with its heights and angles.

Honor it, touch it with awe.
Kneeling beside it explore
its silent everness.
Empty yourself into its form
which has been a star
and can be dust far blown
and is today this stone.
If you should spit upon it,
set it in mortar for your wall,
put it in the trunk of the car
and forget it, it will not care.
But you may feel sadness
in the sun, and by nightfall
immeasurable losses
and in your tenderest parts
the fangs of time.

Mojave Evening

Sundown when the wind turns off
we walk over tessellated sand
to Johnstones' ranch.
They have a well.
They shut the dog indoors
and hose-fill old pans
to water the wild things.
On the cooling earth we sit back
so silent the dreams come.
Is this a conference of shadows
father coyote and his family
around the water pans?
And not far enough to mean fear
only decorum
the periscope ears of three
no five rabbits. Waiting.
A narrow moon steals up.
All shadows are brothers.
Now when the tall ears
bob toward the water circle
we know the coyotes are off
into silver spaces
their eyes coming out to hunt
with the other stars.

Abandoned Anthill

Maybe the gods too
bring gifts
but the city is motionless

no seethe of bodies
bearing, hurrying, burying
the neat crater empty
ringed with grey fur
of the creosote harvest

here's a melon shell
sweet & wet—but—
where are you suckers?

out for lunch?
into another war?
sleeping it off
after the flash flood?

sorry if we came too late.

Two of Us

Skyscraper ears
in the noon blaze
upheavals over the greasewood

diminishing eastward

Jack Horizon-jumper
how happy how happy
your survival makes me

creaking the privy door
scaring you out of your bush
into that fast take-off

Godspeed, skinny friend
like me loner

Yea, Though I Walk

Stunted bush
beside the unpaved road
the shepherd often passes here
with his hundred sheep
their hooves churning the soft sand
the lambs bouncing as they follow along.

We walked under the palms
to see the shepherd lead
his traveling company
but they had gone by earlier
the dust had settled.

Under the stunted bush
a cool hollow in the sand
in it a lamb too lame to follow
a lamb with its feet wired together
lifted its little face.

Did the shepherd plan to return
to that humble patience
that quiet trust?
Come that evening with a knife
his fire several fields away
already building heat
the grill glowing?

The good shepherds of myth
psalm and parable
have always made me uneasy
something wrong there
leading me however gently
to the slaughter.

Second Coming

all the little flowers
fringing the stones
& pale as halloween

dry for a long time now
quiver in the low wind
close to the sand

hanging in there
saving their seeds
dead but not gone

waiting for the resurrection
come again someday
matter of faith

rain

Sonoran Cattle

Thin cattle with humps and heavy heads
black, black and white, rusty brown
unguarded graze on the shoulders
where a scant green emerges
after a scant rain.

Too close to the narrow road
they stand like hitchhikers
only they do not lift their heads
for the car, the truck or trailer
their destination only the next green leaf.

At sundown single file
they trek homeward, inland
by some dusty route they know
black, black and white, rusty brown
duty bound to the invisible masters
whose plans for them luckily
they cannot foresee.

They sleep, they wake, they go forth
a few calves with them
through waste lands seeking food
between the saguaros and the speeding cars.

Here a dark sack of bones and skin
has fallen by the roadside
out of the entrails a raw head rises
ragged wings stir the dust
the rest move on starved and quiet
black, black and white, rusty brown.

Withdrawal

Our dwellings crumbled to walls, to cairns;
The streets fell silent into fields;
Lovers' and children's cries were stilled;
The small statues of gophers dissolved
Into holes like ears in the pale sand.

Once more the world of cities had ended
As time flipped back to an earlier page
Where hieroglyphics streaked the land:
Poems of the wind in an unknown tongue.

No bird to question, no river or leaf
To answer, our population of bones
Rested there in the diamond dark,
And seed in the rainless sand beside us
Slept, and the shrimp in the parched lake.

The hills turned over as if in sleep
While a snore of boulders rocked their flanks
Covering our traces with dolmans, menhirs;
Even the lizard froze to stone.

Yearly the caravans of cloud
Traveled afar by another route.
The wind wrote on, and no man read.

THE
GENESIS
STRAIN

The Genesis Strain

Not sure how I got there,
But a perfect location: smogless,
Free food & 4 unpolluted rivers.

The man I took to at once—
Our bare bodies made us forget
Our parents (if we ever had any).

Adam was given a desk job, naming
Species; I typed the name tags,
Kept the files, fixed coffee, dusted,

Found the best plants for food, picked
Perma-press leaves for rainshawls
& little aprons to keep off gnats.

One super-tree I couldn't believe.
Too good to be true! But try it,
Our friendly next-door serpent said.

That night I served Adam Wisdom
Thermidor made from the super-fruit,
& we smoked the leaves, & WOW!

Adam agreed that was a great
Day in the garden. We felt young
& wise—really on top of it all.

What happened next is beyond me:
Our landlord beating on the door,
Asking these weird questions,

Pointing out clauses in the lease:
No picking fruit from THAT tree;
No getting smart ideas.

He began to issue us clothing
(Dead skins) from the company store.
We were already in debt, he told us.

Nothing we'd done was right,
In HIS eyes. Adam chickened, whined,
"Get off my back. It was all Eve."

After that, hell broke loose.
You should have heard the curses.
Not even Adam had executive clemency.

The snake was sure I'd ratted on him
& bit me. Adam stomped him. Now his kids
Can't play with our kids any more.

We were evicted from Eden Gardens.
Those goons with the flamethrower!
You better believe we went quietly.

Adam found ranching a real drag
Before slaves or tractors; got his kicks
Gunning down animals and neighbors.

Our boys are just like him, itching
To kill each other, & the girls like me
—brainwashed pushovers & finks.

How did I get here?—Via millennia,
Freezing my brains with our meatballs;
Vacuuming my soul with the wall-to-wall.

Tomorrow we run out of air and water.
Holy earth, you need the Maytag
More than our towels do. & A NEW MYTH.

God to the Serpent

Beloved Snake, perhaps my finest blueprint,
How can I not take pride in your design?
Your passage without hoof- or paw- or shoe-print
Revels in art's and nature's S-curve line.

No ears, no whiskers, fingers, legs or teeth,
No cries, complaints, nor curses from you start;
But silence shares your body in its sheath,
Full-functioning with no superfluous part.

Men try to emulate your forkéd tongue,
Their prideful piece dwarfed by your lordly length.
Two arms for blows or hugging loosely hung
Are mocked by Boa Constrictor's single strength.

How dare men claim their image as my own,
With all those limbs and features sticking out?
You, Snake, with continuity of bone
Need but a spine to coil and cruise about.

Men fear the force of your hypnotic eyes,
Make myths to damn your being wise and deft.
You, Snake, not men, deserve my cosmic prize.
I'm glad you stayed in Eden when they left.

TV Brideshead Revisited

Poor Julia, reaching
that time of life,
remembered the beads
in Mummy's fingers,
the bleeding brows
under the nasty crown
in Nanny's bedsitter. Tossed
in that Catholic teapot,
hanging on for dear lust,
suddenly she renounced
her lover and all his works
amorous and artistic.
And indeed, a dull dog he was,
not worth the loss of her pass
to a possible heaven.
He left, morose, no doubt
relieved to be off the hook
of desire over-fulfilled,
however grieved to forfeit
entrée to that stupendous
place that would harrow
his heart through a long war.

Now, over land, over sea,
fans of the TV series hasten
to stand before Castle Howard
in snobbish ecstasy. Surely,
they sigh, Julia repents
of her piety? Charles reclaims
his paramour and her pad?
But Waugh knew well
what he wanted: the True Faith
punishing the illicit pair.
Only by being damned
do Paolo and Francesca live
in Dante's lines, forever
circling the black air of hell.
Sweet endings slip like the beads
through Mummy's hands, like drops
of titillating gore from under
the thorny headband. Still,
reading the book we are spared
the sneer of William Buckley
showing his teeth at the end
of each installment. *Deo gratias.*

Cutting the Cake

Gowned and veiled for tribal ritual
in a maze of tulle and satin
with her eyes rimmed round in cat fur
and the stylish men about her
kissing kin and carefree suitors

long she looked unseeing past him
to her picture in the papers
print and photoflash embalming
the demise of the familiar
and he trembled as her fingers

took the dagger laid before them
for the ceremonial cutting
of the mounting tiers of sweetness
crowned with manikin and maiden
and her chop was so triumphant

that the groomlike little figure
from his lover at the apex
toppled over in the frosting
where a flower girl retrieved him
sucked him dry and bit his head off.

Child as Deity

God in a bib
drools sleep and anger
will not will not
from a silver dented cup
in his fist
imbibe
but scatters milk
batters the tabletop
demolishing
your prayers.

The Wedding Frame

They have survived a marriage.

Behind this barrier of rusty tricycles
worn dolls in deathly poses
supper smells
wearying the morning

Leonard in undershirt, his slender arms
for music built, not labor, smiles
beyond disorder and the untrimmed rose
in the window, the ungainly fruit
weighting his wife's body:

Marjorie: from the wedding frame
a maytime tree tender with lace looks out
her eyes unbounded as a flight of birds

And the years await her.

Here by the careless rose with tumbling petals
in a rented space, "but the violins—
Leonard made them all—" she says; and the young man
courting the maytime creature thrills
at her pride in his slender arms shaping the wood
to music: and so wins her: bride forever
blooming in her frame among the violins.

Now he lifts one, summons three bars of rhapsody
her voice detailing weekend drudgeries
while doors bang open and the children scream
"You did it!" "No, you did!"
guards with her thickening arm
their future, under the soiled skirt

Life in its awkward arc.

Home Notes

The virgin daughter is playing her flute
To the grandfather who once wooed
His wife with this antique instrument.

The paterfamilias on his study bed
Lies stoned. Behind his flaming eyeballs
His youthful typist smiling tells him
Incessantly as the clock ticks that she now
Prefers to couple with a pimply boy.

The chatelaine of the house jots down
"Dry cleaning, aspirin, Bromo Seltzer, bread"
Savors the elegant sadness of Mozart
Compares the crude sorrows of her husband
Recoils from an old heresy of her own
Reluctant to feel in memory that rack
Of silent screams, dismembering farewells
Yet prays, let me shoulder for him a part
Of this heavy paraphernalia of grief.
I also have packed in along that trail.

The notes fall pure as snow from the last
Conifers. The old man sleeps and sighs.
His sorry son-in-law coughs heavily
Slumps easier as the weight shifts to his wife
To long-dead Mozart and to his daughter
Who with her flute distills his foul distresses
Into clear tones shapelier than tears.

Pity Ulysses

Pity Ulysses, fondly sure
his men exulted in their pure
recovered forms and burned to think
what shame befell from Circe's drink.

Be glad he never did awaken
nights when heroes, memory-shaken,
sickened with longing for the sty,
the brutal tusk, the leering eye.

Too Small for Words

Who are these winged visitors
into whose thousand eyes
we dare not look?
One alights on the unfinished poem
one marches across the open book.

Is this the messenger
from thin air who brings
the lens so long awaited
focused on Being
purified of Things?

Last night one hesitated
between the lamp
and my alpine pillow
coming in soundlessly to land
on the white sheet.

Before my mind could follow
a weapon huge
as an acre of hot meat and bone
crushed his antennae
his angelic wings.

Surely this murderous hand
was not my own.

In Nomine

Ovarian vision, wisdom without words,
begins, pervades, maintains, links each with all,
ever-renewing as the oceans breathe
or fragments of lost planets reassemble
and round some central fire new orbits wreathe.

Before the master choreographer
treetops and moons and holy dustmotes dance,
calling across in waves and particles
joined by a vast cacophony of prayer.
Clouds hear and heed the drums and canticles.

In quantum slits of matter and mind and sky
where death is unceasing and irrelevant
the messenger molecules as angels may
deconstruct into pure intelligence,
reborn in the twinkling of a maker's eye.

The soul from its dwelling without doors
can modify microbe and millennium,
goldenrod, geode, godhead, galaxy,
the mountain's parturition when it pours
hot flux entombing towns and history.

My kind, higher than the Himalayas,
a little lower than the angleworm,
who kneel to icons of the human form,
bow to the emblem of Rome's torture tree,
consider: we are one and only one

of the quintillion images of God.
"HIM" we degrade to Dad, policeman, prose,
filicidal, wrathful, one who rapes a virgin,
ordainer of endless torments laid on those
excluded from that last resort, Club Heaven.

Being on whom the priests and prophets called,
Soul of the stars and space between, Pascal
by your eternal silence was appalled;
Yet you are the cyclone's eye, the seedling's heart;
and yours the power and glory within us all.

Corona Fidei

It was that shudder in the soul
between the sex-stir
and a fear of failing
that made the child kill off one parent
re-create the other.

Beneath the sunburnt hair
the skullbones hurt from the gold circlet
that wasn't there. Not yet.
But entering the cool temple
the boy exulted, "A king's house
and I am the king's son in hiding.
Some day they will know me.
All the world will know."

Wisdom so flushed his veins
that graybeards nodded when he spoke
and not as a child nor seeing darkly.
But then, here came the family
with whom he lived: woodworker, housewife,
siblings, to drag him from his triumph,
chiding him for straying off.

"If you are truly my mother,"
he longed to say, "tell me you came
a virgin to my kingly father, and still
undefiled after his golden touch." Her smile
at his pleading gaze was the only answer.

Thus by his 13th year he alters
origins and expectations: reappears, older,
with a leader-look and rhetoric,
healer-hands, miracles, chutzpah.
Romans and Jews of the establishment
shake their spears and phylacteries.

The end is out of his hands,
understandably, if you know the scene,
with the PR men continuing age after age
to search for the best angle.

Children forever, we adore
princes in peasants' clothing,
fostermother wolves, babes in bullrushes.
Family fictions of the great
are our own fantasies, buried in sorrow
just under the threshhold of madness.

Hail, Son of David, Son of God.
Ave Maria, virgin mother (of how many kids?)
Joseph looks up from planing down a cross
and smiles. He gets a sainthood too.

Now We Lay Us

I pray for those who weep
alone on a bed of sand.
One holds a star in his hand
while the desert nightwinds reap
his blood and tears.

                    This leap
we take to an unknown land
(God, can you understand?)
on the farther side of sleep.

Soul travel touches vast
Saharas, seas, and clouds.
Grief whistles through the shrouds
to fall in a bitter rain;
and I am a child again
in a night that may be the last.

Strange Frequency

"We know what his soul whispereth to him . . ."

Sitting at ease in ultragalactic foyers
This sound we frequently hear and clearly trace
Above the creaking of satellitic poles
Above the sleetlike fall of stardust down,
Down through the icy curvature of space.

Not the stupendous murmur of solar fires
Nor the hiss and sting of cinders from the sun
Nor the silver whine of moons swung round and round—
This is a strange and terrible, tiny sound

So soft the ancient light of the furthest stars
Falls not more faintly on the arctic snow;
So brief that a flake of snow in the sun's eye
Outlives this note unheard ever by beast
Or bird, or the wise, antennaed radio.

Man cannot hear it, straining his ear to the ground,
Or locked to his love, though their breath and blood are one.
Listen! His soul is whispering to him now . . .
We have heard it clear as his love has never done—
This is that strange and terrible, tiny sound

So soft, how does it come within our range?
So brief, how can its wonder still unfold?
This is the sound that even we Gods find strange,
Like a tear distilled from the deep eternal cold.

EXIT
AMOR

Where Did I Leave Off?

Where did I leave off yesterday?
I stood at midnight with the mouse
caught in a cornflake box and rustling slightly.
What to do next? I stepped outside
into the backdoor tangle of thorns and roses.
I did not know my neighbors.
They'd be puzzled to see a cereal box
in their backyard. Good luck,
little mouse, I said, as the box sailed
over the high fence.

Our next mouse crept
into an empty cider jug for the sweet dreg.
I stood the bottle up, a sad, sweet jail.
Almost at once she gave birth to a litter of six.
I carried the bottle of mice to Lincoln Park
and left the jug on its side, for easy exit,
under a sheltering bush. They were all
Beatrix Potter mice, dainty and lovable;
not the gross travesties of Disney.

                                    I was lonely
with my husband away all day at work.
But after a wild party Kentucky Derby Day,
we too began to breed in Rapley Caves, under our thicket of
    pipes
but not in a cereal box or cider bottle.

In the first cyclone to hit the eastern mid-Atlantic coast,
we moved to New Haven in such a deluge
that canoes passed us on the Boston Post Road,
and driving into New Haven,
all the elms blew down behind us.
I survived a surfeit of tainted oysters
and gave birth to our first child.
He will be 55 next week.

Why am I telling you all this?

Peeling an Orange

Between you and a bowl of oranges I lie nude
Reading *The World's Illusion* through my tears.
You reach across me hungry for global fruit,
Your bare arm hard, furry and warm on my belly.
Your fingers pry the skin of a navel orange
Releasing tiny explosions of spicy oil.
You place peeled disks of gold in a bizarre pattern
On my white body. Rearranging, you bend and bite
The disks to release further their eager scent.
I say "Stop, you're tickling," my eyes still on the page.
Aromas of groves arise. Through green leaves
Glow the lofty snows. Through red lips
Your white teeth close on a translucent segment.
Your face over my face eclipses *The World's Illusion*.
Pulp and juice pass into my mouth from your mouth.
We laugh against each other's lips. I hold my book
Behind your head, still reading, still weeping a little.
You say "Read on, I'm just an illusion," rolling
Over upon me soothingly, gently moving,
Smiling greenly through long lashes. And soon
I say "Don't stop. Don't disillusion me."
Snows melt. The mountain silvers into many a stream.
The oranges are golden worlds in a dark dream.

Blueberry City

Tiring of cans and paper soups
we left camp for a mythic town
named by an RV captain
as he pulled out, "Blueberry City."
Ten, fifteen miles downhill,
old lumber roads, spindly woods,
I saw into the children's minds
visions of chocolate soda, comics,
kids to stare at, maybe talk to.
My dreams were bunches of broccoli,
fresh fish, summer squash.

Finally a few cars in a clearing.
Hey folks, how far is Blueberry City?
This IS Blueberry City.
Git out and start pickin.
Two caps, a bag, a strange pot
we called Frelenhausen's Hat
from a *Pogo* strip.
Someone warned us, Pick together
and keep talking. When his wife failed
to answer, he saw a bear picking

the other side of the bush.
So we pick bag, caps, Frelenhausen
full, even after the rain started.
Turned back at last with our treasure,
the kids too tired to remember
their earlier Main Street hopes.

The last miles up the mountain
twilit pale with snow.
Camp almost empty, though two girls
rushed past us, calling back
A bear in the latrine!
My daughter nine years old, her heart
on books and bicycles, sat on a log
by the fire between two stones
where our stew heated in the hat
(Frelenhausen's) while the boys
sorted the piles of blueberries
in snow and icewater.
I said to my little girl, Remember
this: maybe the happiest hour of our life.
Snow beading on her dark lashes,
the child stared at her mad mother.
With an icy hand and woolen sleeve
she rubbed at the hot tears
for a future so appalling:
nothing ever to hope for finer
than a trip to Blueberry City,
bears in the bathroom,
stew heating on a hobo fire.

By the Waters

The August of my hysterectomy
I lay stunned in tidewater heat.
My slippery mind swam northward
to bright channels of an earlier summer
where secret bodies of perch and bass,
pike and pickerel hung wavering
around granite islands doubled
when the wind held its breath.

Savage our exultation, teasing
our catch to the red canoe,
the black bass lunging for life;
then the net, the stringer through gills
bloody, and once ashore, the knife
stripping off little coins of armor.
We slit the pale belly, gouged out
the intricate organs, saving only
the roe; then rinsed her lessened body
in water cold as anesthesia.
We ate the grilled flesh with spoons,
picking out bones with our fingers.
Trash, trash to bury in the scant soil.

From a world hidden or half-seen
you grew within me,
water-sister-daughter.
I too have been gutted alive.

Firewind

In September
the Sant'Ana

makes dogs tremble
arsonists go mad
lovers bite in bed

at all hours
sirens howling
into the foothills

along the ridges
rows of hideous suns
at midnight

trees burst

insane deer
run with the horses.

One Ordinary Evening

Lying entwined with you
on the long sofa

the hi-fi helping
Isolde to her climax

I was clipping
the coarse hairs

from your ears
and ruby nostrils

when you said, "Music
for cutting nose wires"

and we shook so
the nailscissors nicked

your gentle neck
blood your blood

I cleansed the place
with my tongue

and we clung tight
pelted with Teutonic cries

till the player
lifted its little prick

from the groove
all arias over

leaving us
in post-Wagnerian sadness

later that year
you were dead

by your own hand
blood your blood

I have never understood
I will never understand.

Dark Lines

My line hold fast and do not break
with drawing life from the cold sea.
I do this for my hunger's sake.

And when I climb the cliff to wake
from hounds of the night pursuing me,
my line hold fast and do not break.

Forget me, Love, and never shake
with grief at infidelity;
I do this for my hunger's sake.

In this and many a poem I make
to sound my dark identity,
my line hold fast and do not break.

Strange food for thought—why man would take
his rest beneath a hanging-tree!
—I do this for my hunger's sake.

Forgive me, Life, the famished ache
to swing across eternity—
my line hold fast and do not break—
I do this for my hunger's sake.

The Ruin

My life's great tower fallen, from base to rafter,
Across this deranged bed with its blot of blood,
Appalling lover, where are the flowers of our laughter,
The bright river of your thought in flood?

The flowers that ringed the tower are crushed and blind,
The warm quicksilver look to blankness turned,
That enormous book of wise, compassionate mind
Slammed shut: bones, rags, and papers to be burned.

Kneeling I touch your unresponding knees
That proved unable to outrace, outclimb
The panic of self, the world's pursuing pain.
Rising I look unseeing through palls of time
On this poor shattered tower that did contain
So long my all that mattered, my joy of being.

Exit Amor

You went out with the turning tide
Throwing a few things overboard:
The bound volumes of our years,
O my dear editor, 1933 to '68,
Promises long kept in sickness and health
A date with Ireland
Barrels of ripe plans
Golden garbage for the gulls
To pick from your wake.

What dark eye smiled from the bore?
What siren sang in the short breeze
Of the ball?
You will never answer me more. Nothing at all.

But forever across the bed you sprawl,
And onto my living heart again, again,
You force the dead weight of that panic and pain
Senseless, impure,
Which you could not contain,
Which no one can explain,
Which I must now endure.

The Year After

In the year after our life ended,
When you put a gun to your head,
In the year that my eyes turned to glass,
That my heart turned to iron,
Only my hands remained human.

They seized the axe for firewood,
The hoe to loosen hard soil,
The knife to prepare the evening meal,
The shears to cut flowers, beauty
Indifferent to its own decay.

Only my hands continued human,
Writing red on student themes,
Writing black on the white pages
Of emptiness. The only tears were black,
The cries were only lines joined to lines.

My shaping hands held up this semblance
Of structure, pulse, and picture
To my eyes of glass, my iron heart.
Dazed Galatea of my own poems
I stepped down from death.

Coronach

In the attic
dust wears your coat
a window of sky
where your face
ought to be

on the lawn below
two crows jab
at a fallen orange
and I cry don't
don't

A Last Marriage

The children gone, grown into other arms,
Man of her heart and bed gone underground,
Powder and chunks of ash in a shamefast urn,
Her mother long since buried in a blue gown,
Friends vanishing downward from the highway crash,
Slow hospital dooms, or a bullet in the head,
She came at last alone into her overgrown
Shapeless and forlorn garden. Death was there
Too, but tangible. She hacked and dragged away
Horrors of deadwood, webbed and sagging foliage,
Self-strangling roots, vines, suckers, arboreal
Deformities in viperish coils. Sweat, anger, pity
Poured from her. And her flesh was jabbed by thorns,
Hair jerked by twigs, eyes stung by mould and tears.

But day by day in the afterbath she recovered stillness.
Day by day the disreputable garden regained
Its green tenderness. They wooed one another. The living
Responses issued from clean beds of earth.
It was a new marriage, reclusive, active, wordless.
Early each morning even in rain she walked
The reviving ground where one day she would knock and enter.
She took its green tribute into her arms and rooms.
Through autumn the pruned wood gave her ceremonial
Fires, where she saw lost faces radiant with love.
Beyond the window, birds passed and the leaves with them.
Now was a season to sit still with time to know,
Drawing each breath like a fine crystal of snow.

Two Sides of the Coin

1. A Dream of Yellow

A thumbtack with a tiny handle
plastic shaped like a slender spool:
the pain when I stepped on the point told me
even a tough heel can be tender.

Last night in a dream from no-man's-land
the yellow pushpin floating by
as if held in an unseen hand
affixed a sadness to the day.

We are canoeing on the Chickahominy
dogwood and wild roses glowing
along the dark and secret banks
your bright hair blowing in the sun.

Now we sit on the dock and ponder
why Carl kept pressing for an answer
and then pulled out when you said yes.
I say, "Carl is a fool and a heel."

After the suicide and funeral
your sister sent me the small brooch
Carl gave you: a yellow ceramic rose.
I wore it in sorrow and rebellion.

Did you send the dream of the pin, breaking
the law of silence death imposes?
Do you dream of the river and wild roses?
Will you shed light in another waking?

2. The Professor Sings of Love

Why was I drawn to my ex-wife the
attorney
and then to a beautiful virgin dean?
Even jogging they both outpaced me.

I drove from Penn to Sweetbriar
where I wooed Kate with my dad's guitar
and the old ballad, "Katie Cruel."

Why couldn't she just keep saying NO?
Entangled in wedding dates and doubts
I began to dream of flypaper.

Then when the great job came through
it was for her, not me.

"New England autumns together—"
she murmured in my uneasy arms.
Already I felt winter on the way.

I wrote her, "I am not Prince Consort,
nor was meant to be."

Ever the good sport, Kate responded
I was witty and wise, and in truth she felt
a bit overage for troths and trousseaus.

Women, like teeth, should be strong
but not prominent.

After it felt safe, I wrote to her,
"The loss of you is killing me."
But even in death she had to be first.

Fair Warning

Parked in your battered Mustang
a little way into the woods,
we watched rain glisten on glass.
I asked if you had written to Leonard.
You said "No, when friends move away
they go out of my life."

Earlier, in our ecstasy,
I thought: Even dying would be joy
if you leaned over me then
in that hour of passage,
your cool, talismanic fingers
touching my eyes shut.

Now, inexorable miles of highways,
tollbooths, drawbridges,
spun before my sight.
Shafts of gear and brake
came between our bodies.
I said "Thanks for the warning."

But I loved you long after
our family moved a continent away,
felt your hands and words
come between me and the wheel,
driving alone at night
into treeless hills.

Midstairs

Praying, thy will be done,
How will I know, I also pray,
What is this will for me, for mine?
Shall I find windows full of sun
Or walls of darkness all the way?

And here on this turning of the stair
Between passion and doubt,
I pause and say a double prayer,
One for you, and one for you;
And so they cancel out.

And now I come to the creaking tread,
Not my way, Lord, but thine.
The steps of grief have bowed my head,
Though it is not a long climb
To the lonely bed.

MAKE
LIGHT OF
DARKNESS

Return to Madison

It is the autumn of 1936,
my bus from the East Coast rumbling
into this place that William Ellery called
"The shining city of my manhood's grief."
I wear a ring with seven small diamonds
and a couple more, a little larger.
I am in love with at least two men, also
the trumpet of Louis Armstrong, poetry,
scholarship, ritual, ice-skating
at 10 below zero, drinking Manhattans,
dancing, Wisconsin lakes and woods,
being in love with almost everything.
A crisis looms ahead: a June marriage;
but 10 months are too endless to be real.
The other man listens for the phone.
We will be walking in Vilas Park
before sundown, and that huge feeling
vaster than the continent will rise
within us, unbidden, unforeseen, and I—
unlike the men I love—never ask
to know what will happen next.
That shining return to a city bounded

by lakes I relive five decades later,
looking up from a Stegner novel just begun,
staring into the dusk of a different time zone.
"I knew that the University was at one end
of State Street and the state capitol at the other,"
and the exaltation of learning, the sorrow and joy
of that year of marvels pierce me:
one all-night blizzard, and the dawn footprints
leaving from my door, filling with fresh snow.

Red Camellias

You going ahead of me
down unlighted stairs . . .
but waking in our window
the lawn green through red & white
camellias, I know neverness.

It was a dream. Nine years
since you saw the sun rise, gold spill
through leaves, over lawns. My face
has grown old, knees stiffen
making ridiculous my love
of racing barefoot.

In the kitchen I drink coffee
eat peanuts, read a clipping:
"Robert Mezey likes it here."
run upstairs to reopen
pages of an earlier world
pure forms, forgotten games.
To survive we must unlearn much.

Lovemaker, wandering Jew,
did you see them plain
my friends, foes, mentors
Gordon* & Roberta of "Kenyon Canyon"?
To be acclaimed young is heady
later on a drag.

The camellias are dropping,
structures & colors come apart.
I salute you, not-quite-stranger.
Poets still coast into day on dreams
drink coffee with the dead
write letters they never send.

*Gordon Chalmers, president of Kenyon College, 1937–1956

For Scholar-Poets R.M. and R.G.B.

Borges, your glorious harvest, grain by grain
my one eye carries antlike to my brain.

Your visions and voice a stirring music start
with answering drumbeats from the hearer's heart.

I could not know how soul in Spanish sings
(heard only on the radio selling things)

Till two translators raised you from the dead,
taking you on their tongues like holy bread.

John Berryman's Winter Landscape

The print of his passage over a white page
summons again the hounds, the folded wings
and the cold hill of hunters coming down
through dwindling trees, never to reach again
the skaters, workers, watchers of their town.

Those trinal peaks he will not recognize
where decades past the snowfields broke and fell
with gunfire echoes ringing his cold dreams.
He does not show us this lone man on the bridge
who stops with his dark burden, as one crow flies,

and beyond Brueghel steps to the rim and waves.

Shirley,

You look over my shoulder as I write.
You laugh like a seven-year-old. You tell me,
"An elegy is strictly for the birds,"
and add, staying just out of sight,
"You'll never catch me in your net of words."

I see your cheeks, rosy as a child's,
your eyes alert with fun, showing us ways
to reinvent our lives, the past undone,
with letting go, trying a new face,
dancing (didn't David do it before the ark?)
You could make light of darkness or deep shade,
turn dullness to delight, watching the world parade,
or gathering friends for picnics in the park.

What happy havoc you will make in heaven!
—Those harping angels at first sight
will know your name, act out hosannas,
choose crazy costumes from old trunks,
join in a "halo, who-has-the-halo" game
among celestial martyrs, saints, and monks.
Nothing Up There will ever be the same.

But stay close by, Shirley, and keep us tuned
to holy everydays; make us define
this numb Thanksgiving, 1989,
not as a bitter irony past reason
but as a season when, with clearer seeing,
we celebrate your life, the gift of Being,
sharing your shining force that will not die,
the joy you gave, the laughter, and the caring:
encircling love that never waves goodbye.

Lorna

Now that I sleep alone
I lie down in a bed of books—
mysteries of Pargeter and Hillerman,
bridge hands, *Newsweek,*
the Portuguese Bible I stole in Lisbon.

The door of the public library
opens on my childhood,
when those scruffy bindings
filled my arms with joy.
Today I was looking for an intonation,
someone to talk to in the night.
So many sad, narrow books of poetry
and not one beckoned
until you, teenager on drugs
in a cemetery, and I brought you home.

Your lines pull me into your world,
Lorna, Lorna Dee Cervantes.
My hand trembles, picking peaches
in your poem where the two hummingbirds
are stuck together.

On your card a solitary withdrawal.
Only one person took you out
before me, now, eight years later.
Come to my bed of words.
I feel like a bridegroom.

Pilot

A man told a story.
He was a watcher of women's eyes.
In the midnight bar he asked a stranger,
"Why wear shades in this half-lit place?"

She felt for his hand, pulled it
below the counter. A stein
winked in a beam of light.

He thought, "She is a prostitute."
She directed his hand downward
to a tuft of coarse hair, a warm mound
that stirred a little.

"This is Pilot," she told him,
"who guides me with pure intent
through my unseen city."

He raised her hand to his lips.
He said, "Forgive me.
I too need Pilot to lead me
around barriers I see too late."

She smiled, groping for the harness
of the dog he had touched
but still could not see clearly.

He envied their trust, their closeness,
issuing into the flash and glare
of her sightless city.

The man who told the story
prided himself on perceiving
from a woman's eyes her mood,
her purposes, and how if he wished

he could control her. Now, he said,
he walked out into the night
aware of a strange helplessness,
a need for the blind woman.

"But I had learned only
the dog's name," he said.

Dover

Dover is 3
his hair like canary feathers.
he puts his blue eye to the hole
in the board fence between us.
we stick out our tongues and touch.

Dover is 5
in a white suit.
mine eyes dazzle I help him pee
at my birthday party
forsaking all others.

Dover is 7
we sit in the tree of heaven
& hold each other like monkeys.
gently he picks my scab.

Dover is 9
teaching me to drink vanilla.

Dover is 12
with a cellar clubroom.
we play slapjack:
my hand under his hand lies
tingling.

Dover is 15	stealing his dad's Melachrinos borrowing cars for nightrides & anatomy lessons.
Dover is 20	flunking out of Duke, drafted. we wrestle in dry leaves. my fiancé races his engine.
Dover is 24	back from Korea & married. his canary crest has fallen. we revisit the old clubroom. my husband is not amused.
Dover is 26	a father but the boy is dark.
Dover is 30	divorced & moved away his blue eyes veined with red his fingers trembling amber.
Dover is 35	& never a day older thin-haired in the satin box with a ruined liver & half a lung.
Dover whenever	I smell vanilla your glazed blue eyes undo me your 9-year-old drunken laughter rocks my heart
Dover come back	to my birthday party in your white suit back to the tree of heaven the hole in the fence

Slow Scythe

Slow scythe curving over the flowers
In yesterday's field where you mow,
My cool feet flicked
The dew from the daisies, hours,
Hours ago! Ages and ages ago
They flicked the dew
From the yellow and snow-colored flowers you leisurely mow.

Strings

While I sighed for a brother
the form in the fastened box
waited out the years.

My father looked away.
Why was I not a boy?

So I had sons
and at last my father smiled.
My hair grew grey
the black box turned grey with dust
and my sons moved away.

When visitors came in, my father said,
"Do you play the violin?"
but no one played for him.

My father died and what could I do
with the closed case of his youth
and the shape that never spoke?

Finally a stranger came
who opened the coffin of the child
without a name
and made a wild singing
start from the silent heart.

I looked across the dark wood
to where my father
stood and smiled.

My brother, I am too old
to learn to play. Back again
into your black coffin.

What will become of us now
your ageless power confined
this room we share
and my dead father standing there?

Break In

Hearing the footsteps of thieves
in the dark downstairs:

what are you looking for?
it has already been stolen
over and over

I listen to my breath stumbling
in the dark rooms of my lungs:
What does it hope to find?
take it and welcome
while I sleep

White Darkness

Whether this is time or snow, passing
Through the night, earthward,
Who can tell—
Each particle only an illusion; yet massing,
Mounting over all,
Hushing the footfall,
Silencing the bell.

"I am confused,"
Said the traveler, "hearing no sound
Though my feet touch the ground
As they are used."

Soft as a shadow on fur
The filling places
Where his footsteps were;
Lost without shape or grime
His path through the level spaces.
How can we certainly know
If this is time
Falling, or snow?

Take My Hand, Anna K.

My mother wept in church, Episcopalian;
Over her far-off town the sun shone bright.
Her New York City child, I felt an alien.
Coming to a crossing the train cried in the night.

My only home is in the poems I write
Who now am exiled by my failing sight.
Words vanish like a flock of birds in flight.
Coming to a crossing the train cries in the night.

Here end my tracks of passion, reason, rhyme
Before the terminal rush and roar of light,
All go together under the wheels of Time.
Coming to a crossing the train cries in the night.

Afterword

In 1927, in the introductory note to his last book, *Winter Words,* Thomas Hardy wrote, "So far as I am aware, I happen to be the only English poet who has brought out a new volume of verse on his . . . birthday"—leaving his age blank in the event that he did not live to see the book published, as he did not. He would have been eighty-eight. I believe Virginia Hamilton Adair is the only American poet—perhaps the only poet—to have brought out her *first* book of poems at the age of eighty-three. But the singularity of such an achievement would be a mere curiosity if the work did not have substantial literary value. *Winter Words,* although Hardy's weakest book, is still better than most poets' best. And I think many will agree that *Ants on the Melon* is one of the freshest and liveliest books of verse in years.

A reader may wonder why so accomplished a writer should first offer her work to the public at an age when most poets have stopped writing. It may seem a simple question, but the answer is far from simple.

To begin at the beginning, Virginia Hamilton Adair was born in New York City in 1913 and grew up for the most part in New Jersey. Her parents were well-educated and cultured people; her father, Robert Browning Hamilton, a serious reader and lover of poetry (not yet an endangered species), was a poet himself, and the author of "Along the Road," a poem that was rather famous in its day—set to music, spoken from pulpits, and quoted through many editions of Bartlett—an old-fashioned lyric, but all the same a skillful and charming one. It goes like this:

> I walked a mile with Pleasure.
>   She chattered all the way,
> But left me none the wiser
>   For all she had to say.
>
> I walked a mile with Sorrow,
>   And ne'er a word said she;
> But, oh, the things I learned from her
>   When Sorrow walked with me!

Virginia cannot remember a time when she did not hear poetry being read aloud or recited. In her earliest memory of a specific work (she is looking through the bars of her crib!) her father is reading to her from Pope's *Iliad,* that neglected masterpiece. When she was a little older, he would recite heroic couplets, stopping short of the rhyme word and waiting for her to supply it—a fine game for a budding poet. More important, she was growing up in a deeply literary ambiance, under the assumption that poetry was an intimate and essential part of life and had nothing to do with worldly ambition or celebrity.

Mary Virginia, as she was often called then, was reading on her own when she was four, but pneumonia kept her out of school for three years. From her seventh to her sixteenth year, she attended Kimberley, one of the finest country day schools in the United States, where she had nine years of French with teachers who spoke no English, five years of Latin, plenty of history, mathematics, and laboratory science, as well as a great deal of reading in Greek and Roman literature—and of course, in French, English, and American. At the age of eleven she was writing weekly themes in French and Latin. She had been writing poetry on her own since she was six, beginning with some "impassioned stanzas in defense of Woodrow Wilson, vilified by my Cousin Rose and championed by my father." A spirited and rebellious girl (she still is), she was often in hot water in school. Assigned to write "on some faraway place," she wrote,

> I should like to rise and go
> To the land of ice and snow.
> I would take a wicker chair
> And sit and watch the polar bear.
> The polar bear sits on the ice
> Because it makes his rear feel nice.

This received a D-minus and the demand that she make another attempt. Which she did, but first she had to be cheeky—"Is Kentucky far away enough?" But she respected the teachers, who were, as she said, "tough cookies like my mother, no rod-sparer herself." And she adored her mother.

Her father was an insurance executive, a lawyer whose specialty was surety bonds; every now and then he would run into a fellow vice president and lawyer, also an expert in surety bonds. This was, as the reader will have guessed, the as yet little-known poet Wallace Stevens. When Virginia was old enough to know who the great man was, she was very eager to find out whether the two young lawyers and poets had talked poetry. She asked her father, who replied, "Certainly not."

In 1929, already a poet with years of practice behind her, she went off to Mount Holyoke, where she promptly won the freshman Latin prize for sight translation. Here too she had excellent teachers, including Roberta Teale Swartz, a fine poet, and her husband, Gordon Chalmers, who was to be president of Kenyon College when I was a student there. (It was the two of them who would bring John Crowe Ransom to Kenyon from Vanderbilt, establish *The Kenyon Review*, and make Kenyon one of the great centers of poetry and criticism in the forties and fifties.) Another poet on the faculty was Genevieve Taggart. Virginia won several prestigious poetry prizes at Mount Holyoke, and in the process got to know Robert Frost, who was at nearby Amherst, and visiting poets such as Anna Hempstead Branch, William Rose Benét, and Wilbur Snow. ("I wish I could take you home to my boys." "Gee, I wish you could, Mr. Snow.") She also met around this time a young Vassar student named Muriel Rukeyser. Her skills in verse were further sharpened by a rigorous year-long course in versification under the exacting tutelage of Ada Laura Fonda Snell, a kind of lab course in which she studied the subtleties of the many different sounds a poetic line can make. She never questioned the necessity of learning the meters and the forms: this was essential preparation for a poet, certainly for a poet of her generation, as it had been for centuries.

After graduation, she went to Harvard for her MA—Radcliffe, as it would have been for a woman in those days, though it was indistinguishable from Harvard—and it was at a Harvard Law School dance that she met Douglass Adair. After she had done two years of graduate work and teaching at the University of Wisconsin in Madison, she and Douglass got married and settled in Washington, where he had been helping to establish the Social Security program. By 1938, he thought that he had enough money to return to school and pursue his main interest, history. He and Virginia moved to New Haven, where he would earn his doctorate in American history at Yale and where their first child, named Robert Hamilton after Virginia's father, was born. (She has a very funny poem about these years, called "Where Did I Leave Off?")

In 1943, after a couple of years at Princeton University and the birth of their second son, Douglass III, the young couple moved to Williamsburg, where, except for a year in Seattle, they would live for the next eleven years. Douglass was a professor of history at William and Mary and editor of the prestigious *William and Mary Quarterly.* Virginia, from time to time, taught literature there. She was not shy about publishing poems, and during the thirties and forties a number of good magazines opened their pages to her, among them *The Atlantic Monthly, The New Republic* and *The Saturday Review of Literature.* If asked why she did not take the natural next step of publishing a book, she would most likely say that she was much too busy looking after a household and caring for the children—three of them by now, a daughter, Kappa (now Mrs. Robert Waugh), having been born their first year in Williamsburg—not to mention stints of teaching and the almost daily composition and revision of poems. There are things more important than a literary career.

But the reasons are somewhat more complicated, as she will readily acknowledge. Looking around, she could see how a young poet, having established a reputation, might then find herself hemmed in by the expectations of readers, who would want the same kind of poems they had found so charming in the first book or the second, and she was too jealous of her independence to trade it for the auction of publication and a passing renown. She wished to write exactly what she pleased and how she pleased, and believed she could more easily enjoy that freedom outside the official literary world. Then, too, she knew enough of the world to see how badly people longed to be known and how they suffered when they were not, how a small fame fed the hunger for a larger, and how painful and corrosive both hunger and fame could be. She wanted none of it. As with Borges, her values and sensibility had been formed to a large extent by her father. He wrote "for fun," as did her mother; one year he read all of Chaucer aloud and even wrote a few poems in Middle English. The house was full of the countless poems that he drew from his deep memory. He lived to be ninety-four and was for more than eighty years both her chief audience and a continuous example of how poetry can sustain a life. There was never any question in her mind that what matters is the health of the spirit, not the acclaim of the great world.

So, with no regret and without making a big deal of it, she chose the private life and the vocation. In any case, no one had offered to publish a book of her poems, and she knew that sending out poems and books would expend valuable time and energy. She simply went on writing her verse, reading, thinking, and, as always, living with the gratitude and appetite and youthful openness to experience that she has never lost.

In 1955, Douglass, who by this time had published brilliant work and was regarded as one of the most distinguished historians of his time, was offered an appointment at the Claremont Graduate School in Claremont, California. He and Virginia and the children moved here, and here she has been ever since. She went on looking after her family, writing poetry, and giving the occasional reading. She taught too, first intermittently at local colleges such as Pomona and LaVerne and eventually full-time at the California Polytechnic University in Pomona, where she taught for twenty-two years.

In 1968 occurred the great trauma of her life. Without any warning, Douglass went into the bedroom one evening and shot himself. That a man with so rich a life, a famous scholar and much-loved teacher, gratified by a happy and vibrant marriage and three bright, healthy children, should end it in such a way was, and is, incomprehensible. In the years following, Virginia came to terms with this loss as she did with almost everything, by writing poems. She poured her grief and anger and loneliness into elegies, bitter and plangent by turns, tender and inconsolable. Several have been included in this book.

Now on her own, she earned her living by teaching, and it was during the seventies, while bucking for full professor—she had never gotten around to finishing her PhD—that she began to publish in the magazines again, but, true to form, once she had been promoted she stopped sending poems out. It seemed more trouble than it was worth.

In 1982, I invited her to give a reading at Pomona College. I had never met her but had seen one or two of her poems somewhere and thought it would be a good deed to feature a worthy local poet. Although she was already beginning to lose her sight, she read her poems to a large audience, some of them old friends, most of them students and townspeople who knew little or nothing about her. It was a triumph, one of the best literary events we had ever had at the college, and I doubt that any of us had realized what a marvelous poet she was. It was that evening that our friendship began and I first suggested to her that she ought to think about a book. A few years later she agreed, and we settled down to the work of choosing from among a great number of poems (though a small number of all she had written) some eighty-five or ninety that would give a vivid sense of her life and of the world and times she has lived in, as well as the range of her interests and poetic style. It was clear that she had no interest or belief in the possibility of eventual publication; as far as she was concerned, the whole reason for the work we were doing was the enjoyment of doing it. And indeed it was a pleasure for both of us, the many months we spent sorting through sheaves of manuscripts, revising, culling, editing, trying to find an order that would add up to a book that was something more than the sum of its parts. When the book was done, we went on spending many evenings together, conversing and joking, she reminiscing or talking about poetry, I reading aloud or reciting to her, for she was by now completely blind, Marvell—her great love—or Gavin Ewart, Louise Bogan, Donald Justice, or drafts of my Borges translations, and sometimes I read to her her own recent poems, rough as they were, composed in utter darkness on type-writer or yellow legal pad. And long before anyone showed any interest in *Ants on the Melon,* we were talking about putting another book together and what a lot of fun it would be. And it will be.

The reader will already have read many of these idiosyncratic, witty and moving poems, with their unusual variety of subjects and forms, and hardly needs me to explain how good they are or why. They speak eloquently for themselves, and for the person who made them. It remains for me only to say how grateful I am for the happy accident of fate that led our paths to cross and brought me the friendship of this remarkable woman.

—Robert Mezey
Claremont, California

ABOUT THE AUTHOR

Virginia Hamilton Adair lives in Claremont, California, and taught for many years at California Polytechnic University at Pomona.

ABOUT THE TYPE

This book was set in Granjon, a modern recutting of a typeface produced under the direction of George W. Jones, who based Granjon's design upon the letter forms of Claude Garamond (1480–1561). The name was given to the typeface as a tribute to the typographic designer Robert Granjon.